Business
From other
Perspective

By

Roshdy Ebrahim, Ph.D

2020

Roshdy Ebrahim

ISBN: 9798606808649

Contents

Chapter 1

The future of business is the "mesh" [1]

I'm speaking to you about what I call the "mesh." It's essentially a fundamental shift in our relationship with stuff, with the things in our lives. And it's starting to look at -- not always and not for everything -- but in certain moments of time, access to certain kinds of goods and service will trump ownership of them. And so, it's the pursuit of better things, easily shared. And we come from a long tradition of sharing. We've shared transportation. We've shared wine and food and other sorts of fabulous experiences in coffee bars in Amsterdam. We've also shared other sorts of entertainment -- sports arenas, public parks, concert halls, libraries, universities. All these things are share-platforms, but sharing ultimately starts and ends with what I refer to as the "mother of all share-platforms."

---

[1] Lisa gansky: entrepreneur, author of the mesh.

And as I think about the mesh and I think about, well, what's driving it, how come it's happening now, I think there's a number of vectors that I want to give you as background. One is the recession -- that the recession has caused us to rethink our relationship with the things in our lives relative to the value -- so starting to align the value with the true cost. Secondly, population growth and density into cities. More people, smaller spaces, less stuff. Climate change: we're trying to reduce the stress in our personal lives and in our communities and on the planet. Also, there's been this recent distrust of big brands, global big brands, in a bunch of different industries, and that's created an opening. Research is showing here, in the States, and in Canada and Western Europe, that most of us are much more open to local companies, or brands that maybe we haven't heard of. Whereas before, we went with the big brands that we were sure we trusted. And last is that we're more connected now to more people on the planet than ever before -- except for if you're sitting next to someone.

The other thing that's worth considering is that we've made a huge investment over decades and decades, and tens of billions of dollars have gone into this investment that now is our inheritance. It's a physical infrastructure that allows us to get from point A to point B and move things that way. It's also -- Web and mobile allow us to be connected and create all kinds of platforms and systems, and the investment of those technologies and that infrastructure is really our inheritance. It allows us to engage in really new and interesting ways.

And so for me, a mesh company, the "classic" mesh company, brings together these three things: our ability to connect to each other -- most of us are walking around with these mobile devices that are GPS-enabled and Web-enabled -- allows us to find each other and find things in time and space. And third is that physical things are readable on a map -- so restaurants, a variety of venues, but also with GPS and other technology like RFID and it continues to expand beyond that, we can also track things that are moving, like a car, a taxicab, a transit system, a box that's moving through time and space. And so that sets up for making access to get goods and services more convenient and less costly in many cases than owning them.

For example, I want to use Zipcar. How many people here have experienced car-sharing or bike-sharing? Wow, that's great. Okay, thank you. Basically, Zipcar is the largest car-sharing company in the world. They did not invent car-sharing. Car-sharing was actually invented in Europe. One of the founders went to Switzerland, saw it implemented someplace, said, "Wow, that looks really cool. I think we can do that in Cambridge," brought it to Cambridge and they started -- two women --

Robin Chase being the other person who started it. Zipcar got some really important things right. First, they really understood that a brand is a voice and a product is a souvenir. And so they were very clever about the way that they packaged car-sharing. They made it sexy. They made it fresh. They made it aspirational. If you were a member of the club, when you're a member of a club, you're a Zipster. The cars they picked didn't look like ex-cop cars that were hollowed out or something. They picked these sexy cars. They targeted to universities. They made sure that the demographic for who they were targeting and the car was all matching. It was a very nice experience, and the cars were clean and reliable, and it all worked.

And so, from a branding perspective, they got a lot right. But they understood fundamentally that they are not a car company. They understand that they are an information company. Because when we buy a car we go to the dealer once, we have an interaction, and we're chow -- usually as quickly as possible. But when you're sharing a car and you have a car-share service, you might use an E.V. to commute, you get a truck because you're doing a home project. When you pick your aunt up at the airport, you get a sedan. And you're going to the mountains to ski, you get different accessories put on the car for doing that sort of thing. Meanwhile, these guys are sitting back, collecting all sorts of data about our behavior and how we interact with the service. And so, it's not only an option for them, but I believe it's an imperative for Zipcar and other mesh companies to actually just wow us, to be like a concierge service. Because we give them so much information, and they are entitled to really see how it is that we're moving. They're in really good shape to anticipate what we're going to want next.

And so, what percent of the day do you think the average person uses a car? What percentage of the time? Any guesses? Those are really very good. I was imagining it was like 20 percent when I first started. The number across the U.S. and Western Europe is eight percent. And so basically even if you think it's 10 percent, 90 percent of the time, something that costs us a lot of money -- personally, and also, we organize our cities around it and all sorts of things -- 90 percent of the time it's sitting around. So, for this reason, I think one of the other themes with the mesh is essentially that, if we squeeze hard on things that we've thrown away, there's a lot of value in those things. What set up with Zipcar -- Zipcar started in 2000.

In the last year, 2010, two car companies started, one that's in the U.K. called WhipCar, and the other one, RelayRides, in the U.S. They're both peer-to-peer car-sharing services, because the two things that really work for car-sharing is, one, the car has to be available, and two, it's within one or two blocks of where you stand. Well the car that's one or two blocks from your home or your office is probably your neighbor's car, and it's probably also available. So, people have created this business. Zipcar started a decade earlier, in 2000. It took them six years to get 1,000 cars in service. WhipCar, which started April of last year, it took them six months to get 1,000 cars in the service. So, really interesting. People are making anywhere between 200 and 700 dollars a month letting their neighbors use their car when they're not using it. So, it's like vacation rentals for cars. Since I'm here -- and I hope some people in the audience are in the car business -- (Laughter) -- I'm thinking that, coming from the technology side of things -- we saw cable-ready TVs and WiFi-ready Notebooks -- it would be really great if, any minute now, you guys could start rolling share-ready cars off. Because it just creates more flexibility. It allows us as owners to have other options. And I think we're going there anyway.

The opportunity and the challenge with mesh businesses -- and those are businesses like Zipcar or Netflix that are full mesh businesses, or other ones where you have a lot of the car companies, car manufacturers, who are beginning to offer their own car-share services as well as a second flanker brand, or as really a test, I think -- is to make sharing irresistible. We have experiences in our lives, certainly, when sharing has been irresistible. It's just, how do we make that recurrent and scale it? We know also, because we're connected in social networks, that it's easy to create delight in one little place. It's contagious because we're all connected to each other. So, if I have a terrific experience and I tweet it, or I tell five people standing next to me, news travels. The opposite, as we know, is also true, often truer.

So here we have LudoTruck, which is in L.A., doing the things that gourmet food trucks do, and they've gathered quite a following. In general, and maybe, again, it's because I'm a tech entrepreneur, I look at things as platforms. Platforms are invitations. So, creating Craigslist or iTunes and the iPhone developer network, there are all these networks -- Facebook as well. These platforms invite all sorts of developers and all sorts of people to come with their ideas and their opportunity to create and target an application for a particular audience. And honestly, it's full of surprises. Because I don't think any of us in this room could have predicted the sorts of applications that have happened at Facebook, around Facebook, for example, two years ago, when Mark announced that they were going to go with a platform.

So, in this way, I think that cities are platforms, and certainly Detroit is a platform. The invitation of bringing makers and artists and entrepreneurs -- it really helps stimulate this fiery creativity and helps a city to thrive. It's inviting participation, and cities have, historically, invited all sorts of participation. Now we're saying that there's other options as well. So, for example, city departments can open up transit data. Google has made available transit data API. And so, there's about seven or eight cities already in the U.S. that have provided the transit data, and different developers are building applications. So, I was having a coffee in Portland, and half-of-a-latte in and the little board in the cafe all of a sudden start showing me that the next bus is coming in three minutes and the train is coming in 16 minutes. And so, it's reliable, real data that's right in my face, where I am, so I can finish the latte.

There's this fabulous opportunity we have across the U.S. now: about 21 percent of vacant commercial and industrial space. That space is not vital. The areas around it lack vitality and vibrancy and engagement. There's this thing -- how many people here have heard of pop-up stores or pop-up shops? Oh, great.

So, I'm a big fan of this. And this is a very mesh-y thing. Essentially, there are all sorts of restaurants in Oakland, near where I live. There's a pop-up general store every three weeks, and they do a fantastic job of making a very social event happening for foodies. Super fun, and it happens in a very transitional neighborhood. Subsequent to that, after it's been going for about a year now, they actually started to lease and create and extend. An area that was edgy-artsy is now starting to become much cooler and engage a lot more people. So, this is an example. The Crafty Fox is this woman who's into crafts, and she does these pop-up crafts fairs around London. But these sorts of things are happening in many different environments. From my perspective, one of the things pop-up stores do is create perishability and urgency. It creates two of the favorite words of any businessperson: sold out. And the opportunity to really focus trust and attention is a wonderful thing.

So, a lot of what we see in the mesh, and a lot of what we have in the platform that we built allows us to define, refine and scale. It allows us to test things as an entrepreneur, to go to market, to be in conversation with people, listen, refine something and go back. It's very cost-effective, and it's very mesh-y. The infrastructure enables that.

In closing, and as we're moving towards the end, I just also want to encourage -- and I'm willing to share my failures as well, though not from the stage. I would just like to say that one of the big things, when we look at waste and when we look at ways that we can really be generous and contribute to each other, but also move to create a better economic situation and a better environmental situation, is by sharing failures. And one quick example is Velib, in 2007, came forward in Paris with a very bold proposition, a very big bike-sharing service. They made a lot of mistakes. They had some number of big successes. But they were very transparent, or they had to be, in the way that they exposed what worked and didn't work. And so, B.C. in Barcelona and B-cycle and Boris Bikes in London -- no one has had to repeat the version 1.0 screw-ups and expensive learning exercises that happened in Paris. So, the opportunity when we're connected is also to share failures and successes.

We're at the very beginning of something that, what we're seeing and the way that mesh companies are coming forward, is inviting, it's engaging, but it's very early. I have a website -- it's a directory -- and it started with about 1,200 companies, and in the last two-and-a-half months it's up to about 3,300 companies. And it grows on a very regular daily basis. But it's very much at the beginning.

Chapter 2

The business benefits of doing good [2]

A few years ago, all the developed countries in the world -- the wealthier ones -- and all of the charities together donated about 200 billion dollars to developing countries in the world -- the ones that bear most of the burden, the heaviest burden of the world's biggest problems: poverty, hunger, climate change and inequality. That same year, businesses invested in those same countries 3.7 trillion dollars.

Now, I get to travel a lot in my work and I'm privileged to see the amazing things that NGOs and some governments are doing with some of that 200 billion dollars: helping malnourished children or families that don't have access to clean water, children who wouldn't be educated otherwise. But it's not enough because the

---

)[2] Wendy woods: social impact strategist.

biggest problems in our world need trillions not just billions. So, if we're going to make lasting and significant progress in the big challenges in our world, we need business, both the companies and the investors, to drive the solutions.

So, let's talk about what business should do. And when I say that, you probably think that I'm going to talk about corporate philanthropy or corporate social responsibility. CSR is the norm today, and it's very useful. It provides a route for corporate generosity and that generosity is important to many corporations' employees and customers. But you know what? It's just not big enough, or strong enough, or durable enough to drive solutions to the biggest problems in our world today because it's incremental cost. Even when business is booming, CSR just isn't designed to scale. And then of course in a downturn, it's one of the first programs to be cut. So no, CSR -- corporate social responsibility -- isn't the answer, but TSI -- total societal impact, is.

TSI is the sum of all of the ways business can affect society by doing the real work: thinking about their supply chains, working on their product design and manufacturing processes and their distribution. The real work of business, when done with innovation, can actually create core business benefits for the company and it can solve the meaningful problems in our world today.

So, what does TSI look like? Focusing on TSI means incorporating social and environmental considerations. And you know what? It's something that isn't completely new. It's been thought about for a while. But the hard part is that corporations almost exclusively still think about something called TSR: total shareholder returns. But TSI -- total societal impact -- needs to stand alongside TSR as an important and valid driver of corporate strategy and corporate decision-making. And we've got the data to show you why and how.

Some companies are already making this happen. They're beginning to make it happen. So let me tell you the story about Mars. Mars is the sixth-largest private company in the United States. If you're like me, they make some important products, like coffee and chocolate. So not surprisingly, one of their most important ingredients is cocoa. And some of their competitors are actually really worried about the sustainability and the availability of cocoa supplies. But not Mars. They're confident in the stable supply of that crop for the long term. And why is that? It's because they partner with NGOs around the world that are working with small shareholder farmers. And those certification agency's NGOs are working to help farmers improve crop yields, they're making sure that they get a fair, premium, livable wage and they're helping them address any human rights potential issues in supply chains, and they're helping minimize the effects on the environment, like deforestation. Mars is on a path to 100 percent certified cocoa, so this is a good program for farming communities, it's a good program for the environment, and it's a good program for Mars, who has solved a significant risk in their supply chain.

But now let's get to the data, because it's actually really awesome. And let me explain exactly what the data points I'm going to talk about are. When analysts and financial people look at companies, they think about a lot of different statistics. I want to talk about two of the most important ones. I'm going to talk about the overall value of a company -- its valuation -- and I'm going to talk about its margin. Basically, the difference between all of its earnings and all of its costs.

So, in our study, we looked at oil and gas companies, and the oil and gas companies that are performing most strongly on

TSI -- total societal impact -- see a 19 percent premium on their valuation. 19 percent. When they do really well on things like minimizing the impact of their company on the environment and water, and when they have very strong occupational health and safety programs. And when they also add in strong employee training programs, they get a 3.4 percentage point premium on their margins.

But what about other industries? Biopharmaceutical companies that are the strongest performers on TSI see a 12 percent premium on their valuation. And then if they're best at expanded access to medicines -- making medicines available for the people who need them -- they see a 6.7 percentage point premium on their gross margins.

For the retail banks that are strongest on TSI, they see a three-percentage point premium on their valuation, and then for those that differentially provide financial inclusion -- access to financial products for people who need it -- they see a 0.5 percentage point premium in their net income margin. Now, these numbers for banks may not seem very big, but in highly competitive industries, even really small differences in margin matter a lot.

Now, what about those consumer goods companies -- the ones who make those products we love like coffee and chocolate? Consumer goods companies that perform best on total societal impact see an 11 percent valuation premium. And then if they do those smart things with their supply chain -- inclusive and responsibly sourcing their product -- they see a 4.8 percentage point premium on their gross margins. These numbers are significant. We've long known that things like fundamental financials, growth rates and financial risks are key drivers of valuation, but this rigorous analysis shows that social and environmental factors -- total societal impact measures -- are also linked to valuations and margins. Wow. All else equal -- we didn't confuse the analysis with anything. All else being equal, companies that perform strongly on social and environmental areas achieve higher margins and higher valuations.

Now, I do understand that companies are under a lot of short-term earnings pressures. But fortunately, the investors who create some of this pressure are actually more and more themselves starting to think longer-term and starting to think with this TSI lens. In our conversations and surveys with investors, 75 percent of them say they expect to see improved revenues and improved operating efficiency for companies that are thinking with a TSI lens. And they're actually starting to incorporate this in their own investing behavior. Last year, 23 trillion in global assets were in the category of socially responsible investing. Now, that's five billion over just the last two years. And it represents a quarter of the total global assets managed in the world.

I know that some of you may be cringing a little bit right now. Because in my decades of strategy consulting with businesses and NGOs and governments around the world, I find that many businesspeople are hesitant to talk or even sometimes think about the business benefits of doing good. They somehow think it's going to negate the value of the benefits they're creating for society. Or that they'll be perceived as heartless or even mercenary. But we really do need to think differently. We need to think differently because the only way we're going to make substantial progress on the challenging problems of our time is for business to drive the solutions.

The job of business is to meet customer needs and to do so profitably. They need to survive. So, one of the best ways for businesses to help ensure their own growth, their own longevity, is to meet some of the hardest challenges in our society and to do so profitably. And when they do that innovatively, when they do that ethically, responsibly, incredibly, they should be proud.

But if you still aren't sure about this, let's talk about a few more examples. What if you're a technology company and you're trying to grow your platform and you're trying to grow your customers? Like, Airbnb. Airbnb has a portfolio of total societal impact activities. They're all spot-on their core business. In one initiative, they're helping enable their community to provide housing for free to those in disaster: crisis survivors and relief workers. In another effort on their part, they're actually helping and working with NGOs to ensure that people can provide housing for free for refugees. Now, what I love about this program is that I don't think most people would've figured out how to express their generosity and open their homes for those in such dire need -- certainly not so quickly or so easily or efficiently -- without this innovation by Airbnb. But at the same time, this is core to their corporate strategy and core to their growth because they grow by increasing the number of hosts and guests using their platform. But if they'd only been thinking exclusively about the return side of things, I'm not sure they would have ever figured out this route to growth, because they're not charging transaction fees. So, it's a pretty exciting way, when they were thinking about how to bring their capabilities to a need in society and at the same time drive their own growth.

But what if you're trying to find new customer segments? Let's move to South Africa, and let's talk about Standard Bank. In South Africa, the government has a regulation that requires all banks to donate 0.2 percent of their profits to small and medium black-owned enterprises. And many banks just donate this to the entrepreneurs, but Standard Bank thought creatively. And what they did is they took those funds and they invested them in an independent trust, and they used that trust to fund loans to these black entrepreneurs. This is a highly leveraged model. They can support a lot more entrepreneurs with capital, and because their success is completely intertwined with the success of the entrepreneurs, they're actually also using the fund to provide technical assistance. More entrepreneurs supported, more people and communities being lifted out of poverty. And it's successful for Standard Bank. So successful that they're actually working on expanding this program to other areas in their portfolio.

It's not like we haven't been trying to solve the problems in our world for a long time. We have, and they're still here. We're making progress, but it's not far enough, or fast enough, or universal enough. We need to flip our thinking. We need to have business -- both companies and investors -- bring creative, innovative corporate strategy and capital to solving the biggest problems in our world. And when they do that innovatively, and when they do that with all of their thinking and all of their strategy and all of their capital, and they're creating both total shareholder returns and total societal impact, we know that we will solve those problems, both profitably and generously.

Chapter 3

The case for letting business solve social problems [3]

I think we're all aware that the world today is full of problems. We've been hearing them today and yesterday and every day for decades. Serious problems, big problems, pressing problems. Poor nutrition, access to water, climate change, deforestation, lack of skills, insecurity, not enough food, not enough healthcare, pollution. There's problem after problem, and I think what really separates this time from any time I can remember in my brief time on Earth is the awareness of these problems. We're all very aware.

Why are we having so much trouble dealing with these problems? That's the question I've been struggling with, coming from my very different perspective. I'm not a social

---

[3] Michael porter: business strategist.

problem guy. I'm a guy that works with business, helps business make money. God forbids. So why are we having so many problems with these social problems, and really is there any role for business, and if so, what is that role? I think that in order to address that question, we have to step back and think about how we've understood and pondered both the problems and the solutions to these great social challenges that we face.

Now, I think many have seen business as the problem, or at least one of the problems, in many of the social challenges we face. You know, think of the fast food industry, the drug industry, the banking industry. You know, this is a low point in the respect for business. Business is not seen as the solution. It's seen as the problem now, for most people. And rightly so, in many cases. There's a lot of bad actors out there that have done the wrong thing, that actually have made the problem worse. So, this perspective is perhaps justified.

How have we tended to see the solutions to these social problems, these many issues that we face in society? Well, we've tended to see the solutions in terms of NGOs, in terms of government, in terms of philanthropy. Indeed, the kind of unique organizational entity of this age is this tremendous rise of NGOs and social organizations. This is a unique, new organizational form that we've seen grown up. Enormous innovation, enormous energy, enormous talent now has been mobilized through this structure to try to deal with all of these challenges. And many of us here are deeply involved in that.

I'm a business school professor, but I've actually founded, I think, now, four nonprofits. Whenever I got interested and became aware of a societal problem, that was what I did, form a nonprofit. That was the way we've thought about how to deal with these issues. Even a business school professor has thought about it that way.

But I think at this moment, we've been at this for quite a while. We've been aware of these problems for decades. We have decades of experience with our NGOs and with our government entities, and there's an awkward reality. The awkward reality is we're not making fast enough progress. We're not winning. These problems still seem very daunting and very intractable, and any solutions we're achieving are small solutions. We're making incremental progress.

What's the fundamental problem we have in dealing with these social problems? If we cut all the complexity away, we have the problem of scale. We can't scale. We can make progress. We can show benefits. We can show results. We can make things better. We're helping. We're doing better. We're doing good. We can't scale. We can't make a large-scale impact on these problems. Why is that? Because we don't have the resources. And that's really clear now. And that's clearer now than it's been for decades. There's simply not enough money to deal with any of these problems at scale using the current model. There's not enough tax revenue, there's not enough philanthropic donations, to deal with these problems the way we're dealing with them now. We've got to confront that reality. And the scarcity of resources for dealing with these problems is only growing, certainly in the advanced world today, with all the fiscal problems we face.

So, if it's fundamentally a resource problem, where are the resources in society? How are those resources really created, the resources we're going to need to deal with all these societal challenges? Well there, I think the answer is very clear: They're in business. All wealth is actually created by business. Business creates wealth when it meets needs at a profit. That's how all wealth is created. It's meeting needs at a profit that leads to taxes and that leads to incomes and that leads to charitable donations. That's where all the resources come from. Only business can actually create resources. Other institutions can utilize them to do important work, but only business can create them. And business creates them when it's able to meet a need at a profit. The resources are overwhelmingly generated by business. The question then is, how do we tap into this? How do we tap into this? Business generates those resources when it makes a profit. That profit is that small difference between the price and the cost it takes to produce whatever solution business has created to whatever problem they're trying to solve. But that profit is the magic. Why? Because that profit allows whatever solution we've created to be infinitely scalable. Because if we can make a profit, we can do it for 10, 100, a million, 100 million, a billion. The solution becomes self-sustaining. That's what business does when it makes a profit.

Now what does this all have to do with social problems? Well, one line of thinking is, let's take this profit and redeploy it into social problems. Business should give more. Business should be more responsible. And that's been the path that we've been on in business. But again, this path that we've been on is not getting us where we need to go.

Now, I started out as a strategy professor, and I'm still a strategy professor. I'm proud of that. But I've also, over the years, worked more and more on social issues. I've worked on healthcare, the environment, economic development, reducing poverty, and as I worked more and more in the social field, I started seeing something that had a profound impact on me and my whole life, in a way.

The conventional wisdom in economics and the view in business has historically been that actually, there's a tradeoff between social performance and economic performance. The conventional wisdom has been that business actually makes a profit by causing a social problem. The classic example is pollution. If business pollutes, it makes more money than if it tried to reduce that pollution. Reducing pollution is expensive, therefore businesses don't want to do it. It's profitable to have an unsafe working environment. It's too expensive to have a safe working environment, therefore business makes more money if they don't have a safe working environment. That's been the conventional wisdom. A lot of companies have fallen into that conventional wisdom. They resisted environmental improvement. They resisted workplace improvement. That thinking has led to, I think, much of the behavior that we have come to criticize in business, that I come to criticize in business.

But the more deeply I got into all these social issues, one after another, and actually, the more I tried to address them myself, personally, in a few cases, through nonprofits that I was involved with, the more I found actually that the reality is the opposite. Business does not profit from causing social problems, actually not in any fundamental sense. That's a very simplistic view. The deeper we get into these issues, the more we start to understand that actually business profits from solving from social problems. That's where the real profit comes. Let's take pollution. We've learned today that actually reducing pollution and emissions is generating profit. It saves money. It makes the business more productive and efficient. It doesn't waste resources. Having a safer working environment actually, and avoiding accidents, it makes the business more profitable, because it's a sign of good processes. Accidents are expensive and costly. Issue by issue by issue, we start to learn that actually there's no trade-off between social progress and economic efficiency in any fundamental sense. Another issue is health. I mean, what we've found is actually health of employees is something that business should treasure, because that health allows those employees to be more productive and come to work and not be absent. The deeper work, the new work, the new thinking on the interface between business and social problems is actually showing that there's a fundamental, deep synergy, particularly if you're not thinking in the very short run. In the very short run, you can sometimes fool yourself into thinking that there's fundamentally opposing goals, but in the long run, ultimately, we're learning in field after field that this is simply not true.

So how could we tap into the power of business to address the fundamental problems that we face? Imagine if we could do that, because if we could do it, we could scale. We could tap into this enormous resource pool and this organizational capacity.

And guess what? That's happening now, finally, partly because of people like you who have raised these issues now for year after year and decade after decade. We see organizations like Dow Chemical leading the revolution away from trans-fat and saturated fat with innovative new products. This is an example of Jain Irrigation. This is a company that's brought drip irrigation technology to thousands and millions of farmers, reducing substantially the use of water. We see companies like the Brazilian forestry company Fibria that's figured out how to avoid tearing down old growth forest and using eucalyptus and getting much more yield per hectare of pulp and making much more paper than you could make by cutting down those old trees. You see companies like Cisco that are training so far four million people in I.T. skills to actually, yes, be responsible, but help expand the opportunity to disseminate I.T. technology and grow the whole business. There's a fundamental opportunity for business today to impact and address these social problems, and this opportunity is the largest business opportunity we see in business.

And the question is, how can we get business thinking to adapt this issue of shared value? This is what I call shared value: addressing a social issue with a business model. That's shared value. Shared value is capitalism, but it's a higher kind of capitalism. It's capitalism as it was ultimately meant to be, meeting important needs, not incrementally competing for trivial differences in product attributes and market share. Shared value is when we can create social value and economic value simultaneously. It's finding those opportunities that will unleash the greatest possibility we have to actually address these social problems because we can scale. We can address shared value at multiple levels. It's real. It's happening.

But in order to get this solution working, we have to now change how business sees itself, and this is thankfully underway. Businesses got trapped into the conventional wisdom that they shouldn't worry about social problems, that this was sort of something on the side, that somebody else was doing it. We're now seeing companies embrace this idea. But we also have to recognize business is not going to do this as effectively as if we have NGOs and government working in partnership with business. The new NGOs that are really moving the needle are the ones that have found these partnerships, that have found these ways to collaborate. The governments that are making the most progress are the governments that have found ways to enable shared value in business rather than see government as the only player that has to call the shots. And government has many ways in which it could impact the willingness and the ability of companies to compete in this way.

I think if we can get business seeing itself differently, and if we can get others seeing business differently, we can change the world. I know it. I'm seeing it. I'm feeling it. Young people, I think, my Harvard Business School students, are getting it. If we can break down this sort of divide, this unease, this tension, this sense that we're not fundamentally collaborating here in driving these social problems, we can break this down, and we finally, I think, can have solutions.

Chapter 4

Your company's data could help end world hunger [4]

June 2010. I landed for the first time in Rome, Italy. I wasn't there to sightsee. I was there to solve world hunger.

I was a 25-year-old PhD student armed with a prototype tool developed back at my university, and I was going to help the World Food Program fix hunger. So, I strode into the headquarters building and my eyes scanned the row of UN flags, and I smiled as I thought to myself, "The engineer is here." Give me your data. I'm going to optimize everything.

Tell me the food that you've purchased, tell me where it's going and when it needs to be there, and I'm going to tell you the shortest, fastest, cheapest, best set of routes to take for the food. We're going to save

_____

[4] Mallory freeman: data activist.

money, we're going to avoid delays and disruptions, and bottom line, we're going to save lives. You're welcome.

I thought it was going to take 12 months, OK, maybe even 13. This is not quite how it panned out. Just a couple of months into the project, my French boss, he told me, "You know, Mallory, it's a good idea, but the data you need for your algorithms is not there. It's the right idea but at the wrong time, and the right idea at the wrong time is the wrong idea." Project over. I was crushed.

When I look back now on that first summer in Rome and I see how much has changed over the past six years, it is an absolute transformation. It's a coming of age for bringing data into the humanitarian world. It's exciting. It's inspiring. But we're not there yet. And brace yourself, executives, because I'm going to be putting companies on the hot seat to step up and play the role that I know they can.

My experiences back in Rome prove using data you can save lives. OK, not that first attempt, but eventually we got there. Let me paint the picture for you. Imagine that you have to plan breakfast, lunch and dinner for 500,000 people, and you only have a certain budget to do it, say 6.5 million dollars per month. Well, what should you do? What's the best way to handle it? Should you buy rice, wheat, chickpea, oil? How much? It sounds simple. It's not. You have 30 possible foods, and you have to pick five of them. That's already over 140,000 different combinations. Then for each food that you pick, you need to decide how much you'll buy, where you're going to get it from, where you're going to store it, how long it's going to take to get there. You need to look at all of the different transportation routes as well. And that's already over 900 million options. If you considered each option for a single second, that would take you over 28 years to get through. 900 million options.

So, we created a tool that allowed decisionmakers to weed through all 900 million options in just a matter of days. It turned out to be incredibly successful. In an operation in Iraq, we saved 17 percent of the costs, and this meant that you had the ability to feed an additional 80,000 people. It's all thanks to the use of data and modeling complex systems.

But we didn't do it alone. The unit that I worked with in Rome, they were unique. They believed in collaboration. They brought in the academic world. They brought in companies. And if we really want to make big changes in big problems like world hunger, we need everybody to the table. We need the data people from humanitarian organizations leading the way, and orchestrating just the right types of engagements with academics, with governments. And there's one group that's not being leveraged in the way that it should be. Did you guess it? Companies.

Companies have a major role to play in fixing the big problems in our world. I've been in the private sector for two years now. I've seen what companies can do, and I've seen what companies aren't doing, and I think there's three main ways that we can fill that gap: by donating data, by donating decision scientists and by donating technology to gather new sources of data. This is data philanthropy, and it's the future of corporate social responsibility. Bonus, it also makes good business sense.

Companies today, they collect mountains of data, so the first thing they can do is start donating that data. Some companies are already doing it. Take, for example, a major telecom company. They opened up their data in Senegal and the Ivory Coast and researchers discovered that if you look at the patterns in the pings to the cell phone towers, you can see where people are traveling. And that can tell you things like where malaria might spread, and you can make predictions with it. Or take for example an innovative satellite company. They opened up their data and donated it, and with that data you could track how droughts are impacting food production. With that you can actually trigger aid funding before a crisis can happen.

This is a great start. There are important insights just locked away in company data. And yes, you need to be very careful. You need to respect privacy concerns, for example by anonymizing the data.

But even if the floodgates opened up, and even if all companies donated their data to academics, to NGOs, to humanitarian organizations, it wouldn't be enough to harness that full impact of data for humanitarian goals. Why? To unlock insights in data, you need decision scientists. Decision scientists are people like me. They take the data, they clean it up, transform it and put it into a useful algorithm that's the best choice to address the business need at hand. In the world of humanitarian aid, there are very few decision scientists. Most of them work for companies. So that's the second thing that companies need to do. In addition to donating their data, they need to donate their decision scientists.

Now, companies will say, "Ah! Don't take our decision scientists from us. We need every spare second of their time." But there's a way. If a company was going to donate a block of a decision scientist's time, it would actually make more sense to spread out that block of time over a long period, say for example five years. This might only amount to a couple of hours per month, which a company would hardly miss, but what it enables is really important: long-term partnerships. Long-term partnerships allow you to build relationships, to get to know the data, to really understand it and to start to understand the needs and challenges that the humanitarian organization is facing. In Rome, at the World Food Program, this took us five years to do, five years. That first three years, OK, that was just what we couldn't solve for. Then there was two years after that of refining and implementing the tool, like in the operations in Iraq and other countries. I don't think that's an unrealistic timeline when it comes to using data to make operational changes. It's an investment. It requires patience. But the types of results that can be produced are undeniable. In our case, it was the ability to feed tens of thousands more people.

So, we have donating data, we have donating decision scientists, and there's actually a third way that companies can help: donating technology to capture new sources of data. You see, there's a lot of things we just don't have data on. Right now, Syrian refugees are flooding into Greece, and the UN refugee agency, they have their hands full. The current system for tracking people is paper and pencil, and what that means is that when a mother and her five children walk into the camp, headquarters is essentially blind to this moment. That's all going to change in the next few weeks, thanks to private sector collaboration. There's going to be a new system based on donated package tracking technology from the logistics company that I work for. With this new system, there will be a data trail, so you know exactly the moment when that mother and her children walk into the camp. And even more, you know if she's going to have supplies this month and the next. Information visibility drives efficiency. For companies, using technology to gather important data, it's like bread and butter. They've been doing it for years, and it's led to major operational efficiency improvements. Just try to imagine your favorite beverage company trying to plan their inventory and not knowing how many bottles were on the shelves. It's absurd. Data drives better decisions.

Now, if you're representing a company, and you're pragmatic and not just idealistic, you might be saying to yourself, "OK, this is all great, Mallory, but why should I want to be involved?" Well for one thing, beyond the good PR, humanitarian aid is a 24-billion-dollar sector, and there's over five billion people, maybe your next customers, that live in the developing world. Further, companies that are engaging in data philanthropy, they're finding new insights locked away in their data. Take, for example, a credit card company that's opened up a center that functions as a hub for academics, for NGOs and governments, all working together. They're looking at information in credit card swipes and using that to find insights about how households in India live, work, earn and spend. For the humanitarian world, this provides information about how you might bring people out of poverty. But for companies, it's providing insights about your customers and potential customers in India. It's a win all around. Now, for me, what I find exciting about data philanthropy -- donating data, donating decision scientists and donating technology -- it's what it means for young professionals like me who are choosing to work at companies. Studies show that the next generation of the workforce care about having their work make a bigger impact. We want to make a difference, and so through data philanthropy, companies can actually help engage and retain their decision scientists. And that's a big deal for a profession that's in high demand.

Data philanthropy makes good business sense, and it also can help revolutionize the humanitarian world. If we coordinated the planning and logistics across all of the major facets of a humanitarian operation, we could feed, clothe and shelter hundreds of thousands more people, and companies need to step up and play the role that I know they can in bringing about this revolution.

You've probably heard of the saying "food for thought." Well, this is literally thought for food. It finally is the right idea at the right time.

Chapter 5

The human insights missing from big

data [5]

In ancient Greece, when anyone from slaves to soldiers, poets and politicians, needed to make a big decision on life's most important questions, like, "Should I get married?" or "Should we embark on this voyage?" or "Should our army advance into this territory?" they all consulted the oracle.

So, this is how it worked: you would bring her a question and you would get on your knees, and then she would go into this trance. It would take a couple of days, and then eventually she would come out of it, giving you her predictions as your answer.

From the oracle bones of ancient China to ancient Greece to Mayan calendars, people have craved for prophecy in

---

)[5] Tricia wang: technology ethnographer.

order to find out what's going to happen next. And that's because we all want to make the right decision. We don't want to miss something. The future is scary, so it's much nicer knowing that we can make a decision with some assurance of the outcome.

Well, we have a new oracle, and its name is big data, or we call it "Watson" or "deep learning" or "neural net." And these are the kinds of questions we ask of our oracle now, like, "What's the most efficient way to ship these phones from China to Sweden?" Or, "What are the odds of my child being born with a genetic disorder?" Or, "What are the sales volume we can predict for this product?"

I have a dog. Her name is Elle, and she hates the rain. And I have tried everything to untrain her. But because I have failed at this, I also have to consult an oracle, called Dark Sky, every time before we go on a walk, for very accurate weather predictions in the next 10 minutes. She's so sweet. So, because of all of this, our oracle is a $122 billion industry.

Now, despite the size of this industry, the returns are surprisingly low. Investing in big data is easy, but using it is hard. Over 73 percent of big data projects aren't even profitable, and I have executives coming up to me saying, "We're experiencing the same thing. We invested in some big data system, and our employees aren't making better decisions. And they're certainly not coming up with more breakthrough ideas."

So, this is all really interesting to me, because I'm a technology ethnographer. I study and I advise companies on the patterns of how people use technology, and one of my interest areas is data. So why is having more data not helping us make better decisions, especially for companies who have all these resources to invest in these big data systems? Why isn't it getting any easier for them?

So, I've witnessed the struggle firsthand. In 2009, I started a research position with Nokia. And at the time, Nokia was one of the largest cell phone companies in the world, dominating emerging markets like China, Mexico and India -- all places where I had done a lot of research on how low-income people use technology. And I spent a lot of extra time in China getting to know the informal economy. So, I did things like working as a street vendor selling dumplings to construction workers. Or I did fieldwork, spending nights and days in internet cafés, hanging out with Chinese youth, so I could understand how they were using games and mobile phones and using it between moving from the rural areas to the cities.

Through all of this qualitative evidence that I was gathering, I was starting to see so clearly that a big change was about to happen among low-income Chinese people. Even though they were surrounded by advertisements for luxury products like fancy toilets -- who wouldn't want one? -- and apartments and cars, through my conversations with them, I found out that the ads the actually enticed them the most were the ones for iPhones, promising them this entry into this high-tech life. And even when I was living with them in urban slums like this one, I saw people investing over half of their monthly income into buying a phone, and increasingly, they were "shanzhai," which are affordable knock-offs of iPhones and other brands. They're very usable. Does the job.

And after years of living with migrants and working with them and just really doing everything that they were doing, I started piecing all these data points together -- from the things that seem random, like me selling dumplings, to the things that were more obvious, like tracking how much they were spending on their cell phone bills. And I was able to create this much more holistic picture of what was happening. And that's when I started to realize that even the poorest in China would want a smartphone, and that they would do almost anything to get their hands on one.

You have to keep in mind, iPhones had just come out, it was 2009, so this was, like, eight years ago, and Androids had just started looking like iPhones. And a lot of very smart and realistic people said, "Those smartphones -- that's just a fad. Who wants to carry around these heavy things where batteries drain quickly and they break every time you drop them?" But I had a lot of data, and I was very confident about my insights, so I was very excited to share them with Nokia.

But Nokia was not convinced, because it wasn't big data. They said, "We have millions of data points, and we don't see any indicators of anyone wanting to buy a smartphone, and your data set of 100, as diverse as it is, is too weak for us to even take seriously." And I said, "Nokia, you're right. Of course, you wouldn't see this, because you're sending out surveys assuming that people don't know what a smartphone is, so of course you're not going to get any data back about people wanting to buy a smartphone in two years. Your surveys, your methods have been designed to optimize an existing business model, and I'm looking at these emergent human dynamics that haven't happened yet. We're looking outside of market dynamics so that we can get ahead of it." Well, you know what happened to Nokia? Their business fell off a cliff. This -- this is the cost of missing something. It was unfathomable.

But Nokia's not alone. I see organizations throwing out data all the time because it didn't come from a quant model or it doesn't fit in one. But it's not big data's fault. It's the way we use big data; it's our responsibility. Big data's reputation for success comes from quantifying very specific environments, like electricity power grids or delivery logistics or genetic code, when we're quantifying in systems that are more or less contained.

But not all systems are as neatly contained. When you're quantifying and systems are more dynamic, especially systems that involve human beings, forces are complex and unpredictable, and these are things that we don't know how to model so well. Once you predict something about human behavior, new factors emerge, because conditions are constantly changing. That's why it's a never-ending cycle. You think you know something, and then something unknown enters the picture. And that's why just relying on big data alone increases the chance that we'll miss something, while giving us this illusion that we already know everything.

And what makes it really hard to see this paradox and even wrap our brains around it is that we have this thing that I call the quantification bias, which is the unconscious belief of valuing the measurable over the immeasurable. And we often experience this at our work. Maybe we work alongside colleagues who are like this, or even our whole entire company may be like this, where people become so fixated on that number, that they can't see anything outside of it, even when you present them evidence right in front of their face. And this is a very appealing message, because there's nothing wrong with quantifying; it's actually very satisfying. I get a great sense of comfort from looking at an Excel spreadsheet, even very simple ones.

It's just kind of like, "Yes! The formula worked. It's all OK. Everything is under control."

But the problem is that quantifying is addictive. And when we forget that and when we don't have something to kind of keep that in check, it's very easy to just throw out data because it can't be expressed as a numerical value. It's very easy just to slip into silver-bullet thinking, as if some simple solution existed. Because this is a great moment of danger for any organization, because oftentimes, the future we need to predict -- it isn't in that haystack, but it's that tornado that's bearing down on us outside of the barn. There is no greater risk than being blind to the unknown. It can cause you to make the wrong decisions. It can cause you to miss something big.

But we don't have to go down this path. It turns out that the oracle of ancient Greece holds the secret key that shows us the path forward. Now, recent geological research has shown that the Temple of Apollo, where the most famous oracle sat, was actually built over two earthquake faults. And these faults would release these petrochemical fumes from underneath the Earth's crust, and the oracle literally sat right above these faults, inhaling enormous amounts of ethylene gas, these fissures.

It's all true, and that's what made her babble and hallucinate and go into this trance-like state. She was high as a kite!

How did anyone get any useful advice out of her in this state? Well, you see those people surrounding the oracle? You see those people holding her up, because she's, like, a little woozy? And you see that guy on your left-hand side holding the orange notebook? Well, those were the temple guides, and they worked hand in hand with the oracle.

When inquisitors would come and get on their knees, that's when the temple guides would get to work, because after they asked her questions, they would observe their emotional state, and then they would ask them follow-up questions, like, "Why do you want to know this prophecy? Who are you? What are you going to do with this information?" And then the temple guides would take this more ethnographic, this more qualitative information, and interpret the oracle's babblings. So, the oracle didn't stand alone, and neither should our big data systems.

Now to be clear, I'm not saying that big data systems are huffing ethylene gas, or that they're even giving invalid predictions. The total opposite. But what I am saying is that in the same way that the oracle needed her temple guides, our big data systems need them, too. They need people like ethnographers and user researchers who can gather what I call thick data. This is precious data from humans, like stories, emotions and interactions that cannot be quantified. It's the kind of data that I collected for Nokia that comes in in the form of a very small sample size, but delivers incredible depth of meaning.

And what makes it so thick and meaty is the experience of understanding the human narrative. And that's what helps to see what's missing in our models. Thick data grounds our business questions in human questions, and that's why integrating big and thick data forms a more complete picture.

Big data is able to offer insights at scale and leverage the best of machine intelligence, whereas thick data can help us rescue the context loss that comes from making big data usable, and leverage the best of human intelligence. And when you actually integrate the two, that's when things get really fun, because then you're no longer just working with data you've already collected. You get to also work with data that hasn't been collected. You get to ask questions about why: Why is this happening?

Now, when Netflix did this, they unlocked a whole new way to transform their business. Netflix is known for their really great recommendation algorithm, and they had this $1 million prize for anyone who could improve it. And there were winners. But Netflix discovered the improvements were only incremental. So, to really find out what was going on, they hired an ethnographer, Grant McCracken, to gather thick data insights.

And what he discovered was something that they hadn't seen initially in the quantitative data. He discovered that people loved to binge-watch. In fact, people didn't even feel guilty about it. They enjoyed it.

So, Netflix was like, "Oh. This is a new insight." So, they went to their data science team, and they were able to scale this big data insight in with their quantitative data. And once they verified it and validated it, Netflix decided to do something very simple but impactful.

They said, instead of offering the same show from different genres or more of the different shows from similar users, we'll just offer more of the same show. We'll make it easier for you to binge-watch. And they didn't stop there.

They did all these things to redesign their entire viewer experience, to really encourage binge-watching. It's why people and friends disappear for whole weekends at a time, catching up on shows like "Master of None."

By integrating big data and thick data, they not only improved their business, but they transformed how we consume media. And now their stocks are projected to double in the next few years.

But this isn't just about watching more videos or selling more smartphones. For some, integrating thick data insights into the algorithm could mean life or death, especially for the marginalized. All around the country, police departments are using big data for predictive policing, to set bond amounts and sentencing recommendations in ways that reinforce existing biases.

NSA's Skynet machine learning algorithm has possibly aided in the deaths of thousands of civilians in Pakistan from misreading cellular device metadata. As all of our lives become more automated, from automobiles to health insurance or to employment, it is likely that all of us will be impacted by the quantification bias.

Now, the good news is that we've come a long way from huffing ethylene gas to make predictions. We have better tools, so let's just use them better. Let's integrate the big data with the thick data.

Let's bring our temple guides with the oracles, and whether this work happens in companies or nonprofits or government or even in the software, all of it matters, because that means we're collectively committed to making better data, better algorithms, better outputs and better decisions. This is how we'll avoid missing that something.

Chapter 6

4 ways to build a human company in the age of machines [6]

Half of the human workforce is expected to be replaced by software and robots in the next 20 years. And many corporate leaders welcome that as a chance to increase profits. Machines are more efficient; humans are complicated and difficult to manage.

Well, I want our organizations to remain human. In fact, I want them to become beautiful. Because as machines take our jobs and do them more efficiently, soon the only work left for us humans will be the kind of work that must be done beautifully rather than efficiently.

To maintain our humanity in this second Machine Age, we may have no other choice than to create beauty. Beauty is an

---

)[6] Tim leberecht: business romantic.

elusive concept. For the writer Stendhal it was the promise of happiness. For me it's a goal by Lionel Messi.

So, bear with me as I am proposing four admittedly very subjective principles that you can use to build a beautiful organization.

First: do the unnecessary. A few months ago, Hamdi Ulukaya, the CEO and founder of the yogurt company Chobani, made headlines when he decided to grant stock to all of his 2,000 employees. Some called it a PR stunt, others -- a genuine act of giving back. But there is something else that was remarkable about it. It came completely out of the blue. There had been no market or stakeholder pressure, and employees were so surprised that they burst into tears when they heard the news.

Actions like Ulukaya's are beautiful because they catch us off guard. They create something out of nothing because they're completely unnecessary.

I once worked at a company that was the result of a merger of a large IT outsourcing firm and a small design firm. We were merging 9,000 software engineers with 1,000 creative types. And to unify these immensely different cultures, we were going to launch a third, new brand. And the new brand color was going to be orange. And as we were going through the budget for the rollouts, we decided last minute to cut the purchase of 10,000 orange balloons, which we had meant to distribute to all staff worldwide. They just seemed unnecessary and cute in the end. I didn't know back then that our decision marked the beginning of the end -- that these two organizations would never become one. And sure enough, the merger eventually failed. Now, was it because there weren't any orange balloons? No, of course not. But the kill-the-orange-balloons mentality permeated everything else. You might not always realize it, but when you cut the unnecessary, you cut everything. Leading with beauty means rising above what is merely necessary. So do not kill your orange balloons.

The second principle: create intimacy. Studies show that how we feel about our workplace very much depends on the relationships with our coworkers. And what are relationships other than a string of micro interactions? There are hundreds of these every day in our organizations that have the potential to distinguish a good life from a beautiful one. The marriage researcher John Gottman says that the secret of a healthy relationship is not the great gesture or the lofty promise, it's small moments of attachment. In other words, intimacy. In our networked organizations, we tout the strength of weak ties but we underestimate the strength of strong ones. We forget the words of the writer Richard Bach who once said, "Intimacy -- not connectedness -- intimacy is the opposite of loneliness."

So how do we design for organizational intimacy? The humanitarian organization CARE wanted to launch a campaign on gender equality in villages in northern India. But it realized quickly that it had to have this conversation first with its own staff. So, it invited all 36 team members and their partners to one of the Khajuraho Temples, known for their famous erotic sculptures. And there they openly discussed their personal relationships -- their own experiences of gender equality with the coworkers and the partners. It was eye-opening for the participants. Not only did it allow them to relate to the communities they serve, it also broke down invisible barriers and created a lasting bond amongst themselves. Not a single team member quit in the next four years. So this is how you create intimacy. No masks ... or lots of masks.

When Danone, the food company, wanted to translate its new company manifesto into product initiatives, it gathered the management team and 100 employees from across different departments, seniority levels and regions for a three-day strategy retreat. And it asked everybody to wear costumes for the entire meeting: wigs, crazy hats, feather boas, huge glasses and so on. And they left with concrete outcomes and full of enthusiasm. And when I asked the woman who had designed this experience why it worked, she simply said, "Never underestimate the power of a ridiculous wig."

Because wigs erase hierarchy, and hierarchy kills intimacy -- both ways, for the CEO and the intern. Wigs allow us to use the disguise of the false to show something true about ourselves. And that's not easy in our everyday work lives, because the relationship with our organizations is often like that of a married couple that has grown apart, suffered betrayals and disappointments, and is now desperate to be beautiful for one another once again. And for either of us the first step towards beauty involves a huge risk. The risk to be ugly.

So many organizations these days are keen on designing beautiful workplaces that look like anything but work: vacation resorts, coffee shops, playgrounds or college campuses -- Based on the promises of positive psychology, we speak of play and gamification, and one start-up even says that when someone gets fired, they have graduated.

That kind of beautiful language only goes "skin deep, but ugly cuts clean to the bone," as the writer Dorothy Parker once put it. To be authentic is to be ugly. It doesn't mean that you can't have fun or must give in to the vulgar or cynical, but it does mean that you speak the actual ugly truth. Like this manufacturer that wanted to transform one of its struggling business units. It identified, named and pinned on large boards all the issues -- and there were hundreds of them -- that had become obstacles to better performance. They put them on boards, moved them all into one room, which they called "the ugly room." The ugly became visible for everyone to see -- it was celebrated. And the ugly room served as a mix of mirror exhibition and operating room -- a biopsy on the living flesh to cut out all the bureaucracy.

The ugliest part of our body is our brain. Literally and neurologically. Our brain renders ugly what is unfamiliar ... modern art, atonal music, jazz, maybe -- VR goggles for that matter -- strange objects, sounds and people. But we've all been ugly once. We were a weird-looking baby, a new kid on the block, a foreigner. And we will be ugly again when we don't belong.

The Center for Political Beauty, an activist collective in Berlin, recently staged an extreme artistic intervention. With the permission of relatives, it exhumed the corpses of refugees who had drowned at Europe's borders, transported them all the way to Berlin, and then reburied them at the heart of the German capital. The idea was to allow them to reach their desired destination, if only after their death. Such acts of beautification may not be pretty, but they are much needed. Because things tend to get ugly when there's only one meaning, one truth, only answers and no questions. Beautiful organizations keep asking questions. They remain incomplete, which is the fourth and the last of the principles.

Recently I was in Paris, and a friend of mine took me to Nuit Debout, which stands for "up all night," the self-organized protest movement that had formed in response to the proposed labor laws in France. Every night, hundreds gathered at the Place de la République. Every night they set up a small, temporary village to deliberate their own vision of the French Republic. And at the core of this adhocracy was a general assembly where anybody could speak using a specially designed sign language. Like Occupy Wall Street and other protest movements, Nuit Debout was born in the face of crisis. It was messy -- full of controversies and contradictions. But whether you agreed with the movement's goals or not, every gathering was a beautiful lesson in raw humanity. And how fitting that Paris -- the city of ideals, the city of beauty -- was its stage. It reminds us that like great cities, the most beautiful organizations are ideas worth fighting for -- even and especially when their outcome is uncertain. They are movements; they are always imperfect, never fully organized, so they avoid ever becoming banal. They have something but we don't know what it is. They remain mysterious; we can't take our eyes off them. We find them beautiful.

So, to do the unnecessary, to create intimacy, to be ugly, to remain incomplete -- these are not only the qualities of beautiful organizations, these are inherently human characteristics. And these are also the qualities of what we call home. And as we disrupt, and are disrupted, the least we can do is to ensure that we still feel at home in our organizations, and that we use our organizations to create that feeling for others.

Beauty can save the world when we embrace these principles and design for them. In the face of artificial intelligence and machine learning, we need a new radical humanism. We must acquire and promote a new aesthetic and sentimental education. Because if we don't, we might end up feeling like aliens in organizations and societies that are full of smart machines that have no appreciation whatsoever for the unnecessary, the intimate, the incomplete and definitely not for the ugly.

Chapter 7

How fake handbags fund terrorism and organized crime [7]

Two years ago, I set off from central London on the Tube and ended up somewhere in the east of the city walking into a self-storage unit to meet a guy that had 2,000 luxury polo shirts for sale. And as I made my way down the corridor, a broken, blinking light made it just like the cliche scene from a gangster movie. Our man was early, and he was waiting for me in front of a unit secured with four padlocks down the side. On our opening exchange, it was like a verbal sparring match where he threw the first punches. Who was I? Did I have a business card? And where was I going to sell? And then, he just started opening up, and it was my turn. Where were the polo shirts coming from? What paperwork did he have? And when was his next shipment going to arrive? I was

---

)[7] Alastair gray: brand protection manager.

treading the fine line between asking enough questions to get what I needed and not enough for him to become suspicious, because what he didn't know is that I'm a counterfeit investigator,

and after 20 minutes or so of checking over the product for the telltale signs of counterfeit production -- say, badly stitched labels or how the packaging had a huge brand logo stamped all over the front of it -- I was finally on my way out, but not before he insisted on walking down to the street with me and back to the station.

And the feeling after these meetings is always the same: my heart is beating like a drum, because you never know if they've actually bought your story, or they're going to start following you to see who you really are. Relief only comes when you turn the first corner and glance behind, and they're not standing there. But what our counterfeit polo shirt seller certainly didn't realize is that everything I'd seen and heard would result in a dawn raid on his house, him being woken out of bed by eight men on his doorstep and all his product seized. But this would reveal that he was just a pawn at the end of a counterfeiting network spanning three continents, and he was just the first loose thread that I'd started to pull on in the hope that it would all unravel.

Why go through all that trouble? Well, maybe counterfeiting is a victimless crime? These big companies, they make enough money, so if anything, counterfeiting is just a free form of advertising, right? And consumers believe just that -- that the buying and selling of fakes is not that big a deal. But I'm here to tell you that that is just not true. What the tourist on holiday doesn't see about those fake handbags is they may well have been stitched together by a child who was trafficked away from her family, and what the car repair shop owner doesn't realize about those fake brake pads is they may well be lining the pockets of an organized crime gang involved in drugs and prostitution. And while those two things are horrible to think about, it gets much worse, because counterfeiting is even funding terrorism. Let that sink in for a moment.

Terrorists are selling fakes to fund attacks, attacks in our cities that try to make victims of all of us. You wouldn't buy a live scorpion, because there's a chance that it would sting you on the way home, but would you still buy a fake handbag if you knew the profits would enable someone to buy bullets that would kill you and other innocent people six months later? Maybe not.

OK, time to come clean. In my youth -- yeah, I might look like I'm still clinging on to it a bit -- I bought fake watches while on holiday in the Canary Islands. But why do I tell you this? Well, we've all done it, or we know someone that's done it. And until this very moment, maybe you didn't think twice about it, and nor did I, until I answered a 20-word cryptic advert to become an intellectual property investigator. It said "Full training given and some international travel." Within a week, I was creating my first of many aliases, and in the 10 years since, I've investigated fake car parts, alloy wheels, fake pet grooming tools, fake bicycle parts, and, of course, the counterfeiter's favorite, fake luxury leather goods, clothing and shoes.

And what I've learned in the 10 years of investigating fakes is that once you start to scratch the surface, you find that they are rotten to the core, as are the people and organizations that are making money from them, because they are profiting on a massive, massive scale. You can only make around a hundred to 200 percent selling drugs on the street.

You can make 2,000 percent selling fakes online with little of the same risks or penalties. And this quick, easy money then goes on to fund the more serious types of crime, and it pays the way to making these organizations, these criminal organizations, look more legitimate.

So, let me bring you in on a live case. Earlier this year, a series of raids took place in one of my longest-running investigations. Five warehouses were raided in Turkey, and over two million finished counterfeit clothing products were seized, and it took 16 trucks to take that all away. But this gang had been clever. They had gone to the lengths of creating their own fashion brands, complete with registered trademarks, and even having photo shoots on yachts in Italy. And they would use these completely unheard-of and unsuspicious brand names as a way of shipping container loads of fakes to shell companies that they'd set up across Europe. And documents found during those raids found that they'd been falsifying shipping documents so the customs officials would literally have no idea who had sent the products in the first place. When police got access to just one bank account, they found nearly three million euros had been laundered out of Spain in less than two years, and just two days after those raids, that gang were trying to bribe a law firm to get their stock back. Even now, we have no idea where all that money went, to who it went to, but you can bet it's never going to benefit the likes of you or me.

But these aren't just low-level street thugs. They're business professionals, and they fly first class. They trick legitimate businesses with convincing fake invoices and paperwork, so everything just seems real, and then they set up eBay and Amazon accounts just to compete with the people they've already sold fakes to.

But this isn't just happening online. For a few years, I also used to attend automotive trade shows taking place in huge exhibition spaces, but away from the Ferraris and the Bentleys and the flashing lights, there'd be companies selling fakes: companies with a brochure on the counter and another one underneath, if you ask them the right questions. And they would sell me fake car parts, faulty fake car parts that have been estimated to cause over 36,000 fatalities, deaths on our roads each year.

Counterfeiting is set to become a 2.3-trillion-dollar underground economy, and the damage that can be done with that kind of money, it's really frightening ... because fakes fund terror. Fake trainers on the streets of Paris, fake cigarettes in West Africa, and pirate music CDs in the USA have all gone on to fund trips to training camps, bought weapons and ammunition, or the ingredients for explosives. In June 2014, the French security services stopped monitoring the communications of Said and Cherif Kouachi, the two brothers who had been on a terror watch list for three years. But that summer, they were only picking up that Cherif was buying fake trainers from China, so it signaled a shift away from extremism into what was considered a low-level petty crime. The threat had gone away. Seven months later, the two brothers walked into the offices of Charlie Hebdo magazine and killed 12 people, wounded 11 more, with guns from the proceeds of those fakes. So, whatever you think, this isn't a faraway problem happening in China. It's happening right here.

And Paris is not unique. Ten years earlier, in 2004, 191 people lost their lives when a Madrid commuter train was bombed. The attack had been partly funded by the sale of pirate music CDs in the US. Two years prior to that, an Al Qaeda training manual recommended explicitly selling fakes as a good way of supporting terror cells.

But despite this, despite the evidence connecting terrorism and counterfeiting, we do go on buying them, increasing the demand to the point where there's even a store in Turkey called "I Love Genuine Fakes." And you have tourists posing with photographs on TripAdvisor, giving it five-star reviews. But would those same tourists have gone into a store called "I Love Genuine Fake Viagra Pills" or "I Genuinely Love Funding Terrorism"? I doubt it.

Many of us think that we're completely helpless against organized crime and terrorism, that we can do nothing about the next attack, but I believe you can. You can by becoming investigators, too. The way we cripple these networks is to cut their funding, and that means cutting the demand and changing this idea that it's a victimless crime. Let's all identify counterfeiters, and don't give them our money.

So, here's a few tips from one investigator to another to get you started. Number one: here's a typical online counterfeiter's website. Note the URL. If you're shopping for sunglasses or camera lenses, say, and you come across a website like medical-insurance-bankruptcy.com, start to get very suspicious.

Counterfeiters register expired domain names as a way of keeping up the old website's Google page ranking.

Number two: is the website screaming at you that everything is 100 percent genuine, but still giving you 75 percent off the latest collection? Look for words like "master copy," "overruns," "straight from the factory." They could write this all in Comic Sans, it's that much of a joke.

Number three: if you get as far as the checkout page, and you don't see "https" or a padlock symbol next to the URL, you should really start thinking about closing the tab, because these indicate active security measures that will keep your personal and credit card information safe.

OK, last one: go hunting for the "Contact Us" page. If you can only find a generic webform, no company name, telephone number, email address, postal address -- that's it, case closed. You found a counterfeiter. Sadly, you're going to have to go back to Google and start your shopping search all over again, but you didn't get ripped off, so that's only a good thing.

As the world's most famous fictional detective would say, "Watson, the game is afoot." Only this time, my investigator friends, the game is painfully real.

So, the next time you're shopping online, or perhaps wherever it is, look closer, question a little bit deeper, and ask yourself -- before you hand over the cash or click "Buy," "Am I sure this is real?" Tell your friend that used to buy counterfeit watches that he may just have brought the next attack one day closer. And, if you see an Instagram advert for fakes, don't keep scrolling past, report it to the platform as a scam.

Let's shine a light on the dark forces of counterfeiting that are hiding in plain sight. So please, spread the word and don't stop investigating.

Chapter 8

How Amazon, Apple, Facebook and Google manipulate our emotions [8]

I do not believe you can build a multibillion-dollar organization unless you are clear on which instinct or organ you are targeting. Our species has a need for a superbeing. Our competitive advantage as a species is our brain. Our brain is robust enough to ask these really difficult questions, but, unfortunately, it doesn't have the processing power to answer them, which creates a need for a superbeing that we can pray to and look to for answers.

What is prayer? Sending a query into the universe, and hopefully there's some sort of divine intervention -- we don't need to understand what's going on -- from an all-knowing, all-seeing superbeing that gives us

)[8] Scott Galloway: The Four: The Hidden DNA of Amazon, Apple, Facebook, and Google, amazon, 2017

authority that this is the right answer. "Will my kid be all right?" You have your planet of stuff, you have your planet of work, you have your planet of friends. If you have kids, you know that once something comes off the rails with your kids, everything melts, in your universe to the Sun that is your kids. "Will my kid be all right?" "Symptoms and treatment of croup" in the Google query box. One in six queries presented to Google have never been asked before in the history of mankind. What priest, teacher, rabbi, scholar, mentor, boss has so much credibility that one in six questions posed to that person have never been asked before?

Google is our modern man's God. Imagine your face and your name above everything you've put into that box, and you're going to realize you trust Google more than any entity in your history.

One of the other wonderful things about our species is we not only need to be loved, but we need to love others. Children with poor nutrition but a lot of affection have better outcomes than children with good nutrition and poor affection. However, the best signal that you might make it to be part of the number-one fastest growing demographic in the world -- centenarians, people who live to triple digits -- there are three signals. In reverse order: your genetics -- not as important as you'd like to think, so you can continue to treat your body like shit and think, "Oh, Uncle Joe lived to 95, the die have been cast." It's less important than you think. Number two is lifestyle. Don't smoke, don't be obese, and prescreen -- get rid of about two-thirds of early cancers and cardiovascular disease. The number one indicator or signal that you'll make it to triple digits: How many people do you love? Caretaking is the security camera -- we call the low-resolution security camera in our brain -- deciding whether or not you are adding value. Facebook taps into our instinctive need not only to be loved, but to love others, mostly through pictures that create empathy, catalyze and reinforce our relationships.

Amazon is our consumptive gut. The instinct of more is hardwired into us. The penalty for too little is starvation and malnutrition. Open your cupboards, open your closets, you have 10 to 100x times what you need. Why? Because the penalty for too little is much greater than the penalty for too much. So "more for less" is a business strategy that never goes out of style. It's the strategy of China, it's the strategy of Walmart, and now it's the strategy of the most successful company in the world, Amazon. You get more for less into your gut; digest, send it to your muscular and skeletal system of consumption.

once we know we will survive, the basic instinct, we move to the second most powerful instinct, and that is to spread and select the strongest, smartest and fastest seed to the four corners of the earth, or pick the best seed. This is not a timepiece. I haven't wound it in five years. It's my vain attempt to say to people, "If you mate with me, your children are more likely to survive than if you mate with someone wearing a Swatch watch."

The key to business is tapping into the irrational organs. "Irrational" is Harvard Business School's and New York Business School's term for fat profit margins and shareholder value. "High-caloric paste for your children." No? You love your choosy mom. Why choosy moms choose Jif: you love your kids more. The greatest algorithm for shareholder creation from World War II to the advent of Google was taking an average product and appealing to people's hearts. You're a better a mom, a better person, a better patriot if you buy this average soap versus this average soap. Now, the number one algorithm for shareholder value isn't technology. Look at the Forbes 400. Take out inherited wealth, take out finance. The number one source of wealth creation: appealing to your reproductive organs. The Lauders; the number one wealthiest man in Europe, LVMH. Numbers two and three: H&M and Inditex. You want to target the most irrational organs for shareholder value.

As a result, these four companies -- Apple, Amazon, Facebook and Google -- have disarticulated who we are. God, love, consumption, sex. The proportion in your approach to those things is who you are, and they have reassembled who we are in the form of for-profit companies. At the end of the Great Recession, the market capitalization of these companies was equivalent to the GDP of Niger. Now it is equivalent to the GDP of India, having blown past Russia and Canada in '13 and '14. There are only five nations that have a GDP greater than the combined market capitalization of these four firms.

Something is happening, though. The conversation just a year ago was, which CEO was more Jesus-like? Who was running for president? Now the worm has turned. Everything they're doing is bothering us. We're worried they're tax avoiders. Walmart, since the Great Recession, has paid 64 billion dollars in corporate income tax; Amazon has paid 1.4. How do we pay our firefighters, our soldiers and our social workers if the most successful companies in the world don't pay their fair share? Pretty easy. That means the less successful companies have to pay more than their fair share. Alexa, is this a good thing? This is despite the fact that Amazon has added the entire market capitalization of Walmart to its market cap in the last 19 months.

Whose fault is it? It's our fault. We're electing regulators who don't have the backbone to actually go after these companies. Facebook lies to EU regulators and says, "It would be impossible for us to share the data between our core platform and our proposed acquisition of WhatsApp. Approve the merger." They approve the merger and then -- spoiler alert! -- they figure it out. And the EU says, "I feel lied to. We're fining you 120 [million] dollars," about .6 percent of the acquisition price of 19 billion dollars. If Mark Zuckerberg could take out an insurance policy that the acquisition would go through for .6 percent, wouldn't he do it?

Anticompetitive behavior. A two-and-a-half-billion-dollar fine, three billion of the cash flow, three percent of the cash on Google's balance sheet. We are telling these companies, "The smart thing to do, the shareholder-driven thing to do, is to lie and to cheat." We are issuing 25-cent parking tickets on a meter that costs 100 dollars an hour. The smart thing to do is lie. Job destruction! Amazon only needs one person for two at Macy's. If they grow their business 20 billion dollars this year, which they will, we will lose 53,000 cashiers and clerks. This is nothing unusual; this has happened all through our economy; we've just never seen companies this good at it. That's one Yankee Stadium of workers. It's even worse in media. If Facebook and Google grow their businesses 22 billion dollars this year, which they will, we're going to lose approximately 150,000 creative directors, planners and copywriters. Or we can fill up two-and-a-half Yankee Stadiums and say, "You are out of work, courtesy of Amazon."

We now get the majority of our news from our social media feeds, and the majority of our news coming off of social media feeds is ... fake news. I am not allowed to be political or use curse words, or talk about religion in class, so I can definitely not say, "Zuckerberg has become Putin's bitch." I definitely cannot say that.

Their defense: "Facebook is not a media company; it's a technology company." You create original content, you pay sports leagues to give you original content, you run advertising against it -- boom! -- you're a media company. Just in the last few days, Sheryl Sandberg has repeated this lie, that "We are not a media company." Facebook has openly embraced the margins of celebrity and the influence of a media company yet seems to be allergic to the responsibilities of a media company. Imagine McDonald's. We find 80 percent of their beef is fake, and it's giving us encephalitis, and we're making terrible decisions. And we say, "McDonald's, we're pissed off!" And they say, "Wait, wait -- we're not a fast-food restaurant, we're a fast-food platform."

These companies and CEOs wrap themselves in a neon-blue pink rainbow and blue blanket to create an illusionist trick from their behavior each day, which is more indicative of the spawn of Darth Vader and Ayn Rand. Why? Because we as progressives are seen as nice but weak. If Sheryl Sandberg had written a book on gun rights or on the pro-life movement, would they be flying Sheryl to

Cannes? No. And I'm not doubting their progressive values, but it foots to shareholder value, because we as progressives are seen as weak. They're so nice -- remember Microsoft? They didn't seem as nice, and regulators stepped in much earlier than the regulators now, who would never step in on those nice, nice people.

I'm about to get on a plane tonight, and I'm going to have a guy named Roy from TSA molest me. If I am suspected of a DUI on the way home, I can have blood taken from my person. But wait! Don't tap into the iPhone -- it's sacred. This is our new cross. It shouldn't be the iPhone X, it should be called the "iPhone Cross." We have our religion; it's Apple. Our Jesus Christ is Steve Jobs, and we've decided this is holier than our person, our house or our computer. We have become totally out of control with the gross idolatry of innovation and of youth. We no longer worship at the altar of character, of kindness, but of innovation and people who create shareholder value.

Amazon has become so powerful in the marketplace; it can conduct Jedi mind tricks. It can begin damaging other industries just by looking at them. Nike announces they're distributing on Amazon, their stock goes up, every other footwear stock goes down. When Amazon stock goes up, the rest of retail stocks go down, because they assume what's good for Amazon is bad for everybody else. They cut the cost on salmon 33 percent when they acquired Whole Foods. In between the time they announced the acquisition of Whole Foods and when it closed, Kroger, the largest pure-play grocer in America, shed a third of its value, because Amazon purchased a grocer one-eleventh the size of Kroger.

I got very lucky. I predicted the acquisition of Whole Foods by Amazon the week before it happened. This is me boasting; I said this publicly in the media. This was the largest acquisition in their history, they'd never made an acquisition over a billion, and people asked, "How did you know this?" So I'm letting this very impressive audience in on the secret. How did I know this? I'm going to tell you how I knew. I bark at Alexa all day long and try to figure out what's going on.

Alexa, buy whole milk. (Alexa) I couldn't find anything for whole milk, so I've added whole milk to your shopping list. Then I asked, Alexa, buy organic foods. (Alexa) The top search result for organic food is Plum Organics baby food, banana and pumpkin, 12-pack of four ounces each. It's 15 dollars total. Would you like to buy it? And then, as often happens at my age, I got confused. Alexa, buy whole foods. (Alexa) I have purchased the outstanding stock of Whole Foods Incorporated at 42 dollars per share. I have charged 13.7 billion to your American Express card.

We've personified these companies, and just as when you're really angry over every little thing someone does in your life and relationships, you've got to ask yourself, "What's going on here? Why are we so disappointed in technology?" I believe it's because the ratio of one-percent pursuit of shareholder value and 99 percent the betterment of humanity that technology used to play has been flipped, and now we're totally focused on shareholder value instead of humanity.

One hundred thousand people came together for the Manhattan Project and literally saved the world. Technology saved the world. My mother was a four-year-old Jew living in London at the outset of the war. If we had not won the footrace towards splitting the atom, would she have survived? It's unlikely. Twenty-five years later, the most impressive accomplishment, arguably, ever in all of humankind: put a man on the moon. Four hundred thirty thousand Canadians, British and

Americans came together, again, with very basic technology, and put a man on the moon.

Now we have the 700,000 best and brightest, and these are the best and brightest from the four corners of the earth. They are literally playing with lasers relative to slingshots, relative to the squirt gun. They have the GDP of India to work at. And after studying these companies for 10 years, I know what their mission is. Is it to organize the world's information? Is it to connect us? Is it to create greater comity of man? It isn't. I know why we have brought together -- I know that the greatest collection of IQ capital and creativity, that their sole mission is: to sell another fucking Nissan.

Chapter 9

How a handful of tech companies control billions of minds every day [9]

I want you to imagine walking into a room, a control room with a bunch of people, a hundred people, hunched over a desk with little dials, and that that control room will shape the thoughts and feelings of a billion people. This might sound like science fiction, but this actually exists right now, today.

I know because I used to be in one of those control rooms. I was a design ethicist at Google, where I studied how do you ethically steer people's thoughts? Because what we don't talk about is how the handful of people working at a handful of technology companies through their choices will steer what a billion people are thinking today. Because when you pull out your phone and they design how this works or what's

---

)[9] Tristan harris: design thinker.

on the feed, it's scheduling little blocks of time in our minds. If you see a notification, it schedules you to have thoughts that maybe you didn't intend to have. If you swipe over that notification, it schedules you into spending a little bit of time getting sucked into something that maybe you didn't intend to get sucked into. When we talk about technology, we tend to talk about it as this blue-sky opportunity. It could go any direction. And I want to get serious for a moment and tell you why it's going in a very specific direction. Because it's not evolving randomly. There's a hidden goal driving the direction of all of the technology we make, and that goal is the race for our attention. Because every news site, elections, politicians, games, even meditation apps have to compete for one thing, which is our attention, and there's only so much of it. And the best way to get people's attention is to know how someone's mind works. And there's a whole bunch of persuasive techniques that I learned in college at a lab called the Persuasive Technology Lab to get people's attention.

A simple example is YouTube. YouTube wants to maximize how much time you spend. And so what do they do? They autoplay the next video. And let's say that works really well. They're getting a little bit more of people's time. Well, if you're Netflix, you look at that and say, well, that's shrinking my market share, so I'm going to autoplay the next episode. But then if you're Facebook, you say, that's shrinking all of my market share, so now I have to autoplay all the videos in the newsfeed before waiting for you to click play. So, the internet is not evolving at random. The reason it feels like it's sucking us in the way it is because of this race for attention. We know where this is going. Technology is not neutral, and it becomes this race to the bottom of the brain stem of who can go lower to get it.

Let me give you an example of Snapchat. If you didn't know, Snapchat is the number one way that teenagers in the United States communicate. So, if you're like me, and you use text messages to communicate, Snapchat is that for teenagers, and there's, like, a hundred million of them that use it. And they invented a feature called Snapstreaks, which shows the number of days in a row that two people have communicated with each other. In other words, what they just did is they gave two people something they don't want to lose. Because if you're a teenager, and you have 150 days in a row, you don't want that to go away. And so think of the little blocks of time that that schedules in kids' minds. This isn't theoretical: when kids go on vacation, it's been shown they give their passwords to up to five other friends to keep their Snapstreaks going, even when they can't do it. And they have, like, 30 of these things, and so they have to get through taking photos of just pictures or walls or ceilings just to get through their day. So, it's not even like they're having real conversations. We have a temptation to think about this as, oh, they're just using Snapchat the way we used to gossip on the telephone. It's probably OK. Well, what this miss is that in the 1970s, when you were just gossiping on the telephone, there wasn't a hundred engineers on the other side of the screen who knew exactly how your psychology worked and orchestrated you into a double bind with each other.

Now, if this is making you feel a little bit of outrage, notice that that thought just comes over you. Outrage is a really good way also of getting your attention, because we don't choose outrage. It happens to us. And if you're the Facebook newsfeed, whether you'd want to or not, you actually benefit when there's outrage. Because outrage doesn't just schedule a reaction in emotional time, space, for you. We want to share that outrage with other people. So we want to hit share and say, "Can you believe the thing that they said?" And so outrage works really well at getting attention, such that if Facebook had a choice between showing you the outrage feed and a calm newsfeed, they would want to show you the outrage feed, not because someone consciously chose that, but because that worked better at getting your attention. And the newsfeed control room is not accountable to us. It's only accountable to maximizing attention. It's also accountable, because of the business model of advertising, for anybody who can pay the most to actually walk into the control room and say, "That group over there, I want to schedule these thoughts into their minds." So you can target, you can precisely target a lie directly to the people who are most susceptible. And because this is profitable, it's only going to get worse.

So, I'm here today because the costs are so obvious. I don't know a more urgent problem than this, because this problem is underneath all other problems. It's not just taking away our agency to spend our attention and live the lives that we want, it's changing the way that we have our conversations, it's changing our democracy, and it's changing our ability to have the conversations and relationships we want with each other. And it affects everyone, because a billion people have one of these in their pocket.

So how do we fix this? We need to make three radical changes to technology and to our society. The first is we need to acknowledge that we are persuadable. Once you start understanding that your mind can be scheduled into having little thoughts or little blocks of time that you didn't choose, wouldn't we want to use that understanding and protect against the way that that happens? I think we need to see ourselves fundamentally in a new way. It's almost liked a new period of human history, like the Enlightenment, but almost a kind of self-aware Enlightenment, that we can be persuaded, and there might be something we want to protect. The second is we need new models and accountability systems so that as the world gets better and more and more persuasive over time -- because it's only going to get more persuasive -- that the people in those control rooms are accountable and transparent to what we want. The only form of ethical persuasion that exists is when the goals of the persuader are aligned with the goals of the persuadee. And that involves questioning big things, like the business model of advertising. Lastly, we need a design renaissance, because once you have this view of human nature, that you can steer the timelines of a billion people -- just imagine, there's people who have some desire about what they want to do and what they want to be thinking and what they want to be feeling and how they want to be informed, and we're all just tugged into these other directions. And you have a billion people just tugged into all these different directions. Well, imagine an entire design renaissance that tried to orchestrate the exact and most empowering time-well-spent way for those timelines to happen. And that would involve two things: one would be protecting against the timelines that we don't want to be experiencing, the thoughts that we wouldn't want to be happening, so that when that ding happens, not having the ding that sends us away; and the second would be empowering us to live out the timeline that we want.

So, let me give you a concrete example. Today, let's say your friend cancels dinner on you, and you are feeling a little bit lonely. And so, what do you do in that moment? You open up Facebook.

And in that moment, the designers in the control room want to schedule exactly one thing, which is to maximize how much time you spend on the screen. Now, instead, imagine if those designers created a different timeline that was the easiest way, using all of their data, to actually help you get out with the people that you care about? Just think, alleviating all loneliness in society, if that was the timeline that Facebook wanted to make possible for people. Or imagine a different conversation. Let's say you wanted to post something supercontroversial on Facebook, which is a really important thing to be able to do, to talk about controversial topics.

And right now, when there's that big comment box, it's almost asking you, what key do you want to type? In other words, it's scheduling a little timeline of things you're going to continue to do on the screen. And imagine instead that there was another button there saying, what would be most time well spent for you? And you click "host a dinner." And right there underneath the item it said, "Who wants to RSVP for the dinner?" And so, you'd still have a conversation about something controversial, but you'd be having it in the most empowering place on your timeline, which would be at home that night with a bunch of a friends over to talk about it. So imagine we're running, like, a find and replace on all of the timelines that are currently steering us towards more and more screen time persuasively and replacing all of those timelines with what do we want in our lives.

It doesn't have to be this way. Instead of handicapping our attention, imagine if we used all of this data and all of this power and this new view of human nature to give us a superhuman ability to focus and a superhuman ability to put our attention to what we cared about and a superhuman ability to have the conversations that we need to have for democracy. The most complex challenges in the world require not just us to use our attention individually. They require us to use our attention and coordinate it together. Climate change is going to require that a lot of people are being able to coordinate their attention in the most empowering way together. And imagine creating a superhuman ability to do that.

Sometimes the world's most pressing and important problems are not these hypothetical future things that we could create in the future. Sometimes the most pressing problems are the ones that are right underneath our noses, the things that are already directing a billion people's thoughts. And maybe instead of getting excited about the new augmented reality and virtual reality and these cool things that could happen, which are going to be susceptible to the same race for attention, if we could fix the race for attention on the thing that's already in a billion people's pockets. Maybe instead of getting excited about the most exciting new cool fancy education apps, we could fix the way kids' minds are getting manipulated into sending empty messages back and forth.

Maybe instead of worrying about hypothetical future runaway artificial intelligences that are maximizing for one goal, we could solve the runaway artificial intelligence that already exists right now, which are these newsfeeds maximizing for one thing. It's almost like instead of running away to colonize new planets, we could fix the one that we're already on.

Solving this problem is critical infrastructure for solving every other problem. There's nothing in your life or in our collective problems that does not require our ability to put our attention where we care about. At the end of our lives, all we have is our attention and our time. What will be time well spent for ours?

Chapter 10

The future we're building [10]

We're trying to dig a hole under LA, and this is to create the beginning of what will hopefully be a 3D network of tunnels to alleviate congestion. So right now, one of the most soul-destroying things is traffic. It affects people in every part of the world. It takes away so much of your life. It's horrible. It's particularly horrible in LA.

to show what we're talking about. So, a couple of key things that are important in having a 3D tunnel network. First of all, you have to be able to integrate the entrance and exit of the tunnel seamlessly into the fabric of the city. So, by having an elevator, sort of a car skate, that's on an elevator, you can integrate the entrance and exits to the tunnel network just by using two parking spaces. And then the car gets

---

)[10] Elon musk: CEO and product architect of tesla motors, CEO of space x.

on a skate. There's no speed limit here, so we're designing this to be able to operate at 200 kilometers an hour, or about 130 miles per hour. So, you should be able to get from, say, Westwood to LAX in six minutes -- five, six minutes.

there's no real limit to how many levels of tunnel you can have. You can go much further deep than you can go up. The deepest mines are much deeper than the tallest buildings are tall, so you can alleviate any arbitrary level of urban congestion with a 3D tunnel network. This is a very important point. So, a key rebuttal to the tunnels is that if you add one layer of tunnels, that will simply alleviate congestion, it will get used up, and then you'll be back where you started, back with congestion. But you can go to any arbitrary number of tunnels, any number of levels.

To give you an example, the LA subway extension, which is -- I think it's a two-and-a-half-mile   extension that   was   just completed for two billion dollars. So, it's roughly a billion dollars a mile to do the subway extension in LA. And this is not the highest utility subway in the world. So yeah, it's quite difficult to dig tunnels normally. I think we need to have at least a tenfold improvement in the cost per mile of tunneling.

Actually, if you just do two things, you can get to approximately an order of magnitude improvement, and I think you can go beyond that. So, the first thing to do is to cut the tunnel diameter by a factor of two or more. So, a single road lane tunnel according to regulations has to be 26 feet, maybe 28 feet in diameter to allow for crashes and emergency vehicles and sufficient ventilation for combustion engine cars. But if you shrink that diameter to what we're attempting, which is 12 feet, which is plenty to get an electric skate through, you drop the diameter by a factor of two and the cross-sectional area by a factor of four, and the tunneling cost scales with the cross-sectional area. So that's roughly a half-order of magnitude improvement right there. Then tunneling machines currently tunnel for half the time, then they stop, and then the rest of the time is putting in reinforcements for the tunnel wall. So, if you design the machine instead to do continuous tunneling and reinforcing, that will give you a factor of two improvement. Combine that and that's a factor of eight. Also, these machines are far from being at their power or thermal limits, so you can jack up the power to the machine substantially. I think you can get at least a factor of two, maybe a factor of four or five improvement on top of that. So I think there's a fairly straightforward series of steps to get somewhere in excess of an order of magnitude improvement in the cost per mile, and our target actually is -- we've got a pet snail called Gary, this is from Gary the snail from "South Park," I mean, sorry, "SpongeBob SquarePants." currently he's capable of going 14 times faster than a tunnel-boring machine.

I'm in favor of flying things. Obviously, I do rockets, so I like things that fly. This is not some inherent bias against flying things, but there is a challenge with flying cars in that they'll be quite noisy, the wind force generated will be very high. Let's just say that if something's flying over your head, a whole bunch of flying cars going all over the place, that is not an anxiety-reducing situation.

You don't think to yourself, "Well, I feel better about today." You're thinking, "Did they service their hubcap, or is it going to come off and guillotine me?" Things like that.

we've been sort of puttering around with the Hyperloop stuff for a while. We built a Hyperloop test track adjacent to SpaceX, just for a student competition, to encourage innovative ideas in transport. And it actually ends up being the biggest vacuum chamber in the world after the Large Hadron Collider, by volume. So it was quite fun to do that, but it was kind of a hobby thing, and then we think we might -- so we've built a little pusher car to push the student pods, but we're going to try seeing how fast we can make the pusher go if it's not pushing something. So, we're cautiously optimistic we'll be able to be faster than the world's fastest bullet train even in a .8-mile stretch.

looking at tunneling technology, it turns out that in order to make a tunnel, you have to -- In order to seal against the water table, you've got to typically design a tunnel wall to be good to about five or six atmospheres. So, to go to vacuum is only one atmosphere, or near-vacuum. So actually, it sorts of turns out that automatically, if you build a tunnel that is good enough to resist the water table, it is automatically capable of holding vacuum.

I think there's no real length limit. You could dig as much as you want. I think if you were to do something like a DC-to-New York Hyperloop, I think you'd probably want to go underground the entire way because it's a high-density area. You're going under a lot of buildings and houses, and if you go deep enough, you cannot detect the tunnel. Sometimes people think, well, it's going to be pretty annoying to have a tunnel dug under my house. Like, if that tunnel is dug more than about three or four tunnel diameters beneath your house, you will not be able to detect it being dug at all. In fact, if you're able to detect the tunnel being dug, whatever device you are using, you can get a lot of money for that device from the Israeli military, who is trying to detect tunnels from Hamas, and from the US Customs and Border patrol that try and detect drug tunnels. So the reality is that earth is incredibly good at absorbing vibrations, and once the tunnel depth is below a certain level, it is undetectable. Maybe if you have a very sensitive seismic instrument, you might be able to detect it.

A lot of people think that when you make cars autonomous, they'll be able to go faster and that will alleviate congestion. And to some degree that will be true, but once you have shared autonomy where it's much cheaper to go by car and you can go point to point, the affordability of going in a car will be better than that of a bus. Like, it will cost less than a bus ticket. So, the amount of driving that will occur will be much greater with shared autonomy, and actually traffic will get far worse.

I think almost every automaker has some electric vehicle program. They vary in seriousness. Some are very serious about transitioning entirely to electric, and some are just dabbling in it. And some, amazingly, are still pursuing fuel cells, but I think that won't last much longer.

I intend to stay with Tesla as far into the future as I can imagine, and there are a lot of exciting things that we have coming. Obviously, the Model 3 is coming soon. We'll be unveiling the Tesla Semi truck.

so, this is using only cameras and GPS. So, there's no LIDAR or radar being used here. This is just using passive optical, which is essentially what a person uses. The whole road system is meant to be navigated with passive optical, or cameras, and so once you solve cameras or vision, then autonomy is solved. If you don't solve vision, it's not solved. So that's why our focus is so heavily on having a vision neural net that's very effective for road conditions.

You can absolutely be superhuman with just cameras. Like, you can probably do it ten times better than humans would, just cameras. I think we're still on track for being able to go cross-country from LA to New York by the end of the year, fully autonomous.

Essentially, November or December of this year, we should be able to go all the way from a parking lot in California to a parking lot in New York, no controls touched at any point during the entire journey.

but the thing that will be interesting is that I'm actually fairly confident it will be able to do that route even if you change the route dynamically. So, it's fairly easy -- If you say I'm going to be really good at one specific route, that's one thing, but it should be able to go, really be very good, certainly once you enter a highway, to go anywhere on the highway system in a given country. So, it's not sorts of limited to LA to New York. We could change it and make it Seattle-Florida, that day, in real time. So, you were going from LA to New York. Now go from LA to Toronto.

So, the real trick of it is not how do you make it work say 99.9 percent of the time, because, like, if a car crashes one in a thousand times, then you're probably still not going to be comfortable falling asleep. You shouldn't be, certainly.

It's never going to be perfect. No system is going to be perfect, but if you say it's perhaps -- the car is unlikely to crash in a hundred lifetimes, or a thousand lifetimes, then people are like, OK, wow, if I were to live a thousand lives, I would still most likely never experience a crash, then that's probably OK.

the autonomy system is likely to at least mitigate the crash, except in rare circumstances. The thing to appreciate about vehicle safety is this is probabilistic. I mean, there's some chance that any time a human driver gets in a car, that they will have an accident that is their fault. It's never zero. So really the key threshold for autonomy is how much better does autonomy need to be than a person before you can rely on it?

there will be a shared autonomy fleet where you buy your car and you can choose to use that car exclusively, you could choose to have it be used only by friends and family, only by other drivers who are rated five star, you can choose to share it sometimes but no other times. That's 100 percent what will occur. It's just a question of when.

this is a heavy duty, long-range semitruck. So, it's the highest weight capability and with long range. So essentially, it's meant to alleviate the heavy-duty trucking loads. And this is something which people do not today think is possible. They think the truck doesn't have enough power or it doesn't have enough range, and then with the Tesla Semi we want to show that no, an electric truck actually can out-torque any diesel semi. And if you had a tug-of-war competition, the Tesla Semi will tug the diesel semi uphill.

what will be really fun about this is you have a flat torque RPM curve with an electric motor, whereas with a diesel motor or any kind of internal combustion engine car, you've got a torque RPM curve that looks like a hill. So, this will be a very spry truck. You can drive this around like a sports car. There's no gears. It's, like, single speed.

It's quite bizarre test-driving. When I was driving the test prototype for the first truck. It's really weird, because you're driving around and you're just so nimble, and you're in this giant truck. It's just like, driving this giant truck and making these mad maneuvers.

We're very confident that the cost of the roof plus the cost of electricity -- A solar glass roof will be less than the cost of a normal roof plus the cost of electricity. So, in other words, this will be economically a no-brainer, we think it will look great, and it will last -- We thought about having the warranty be infinity, but then people thought, well, that might sound like were just talking rubbish, but actually this is toughened glass. Well after the house has collapsed and there's nothing there, the glass tiles will still be there.

eventually almost all houses will have a solar roof. The thing is to consider the time scale here to be probably on the order of 40 or 50 years. So, on average, a roof is replaced every 20 to 25 years. But you don't start replacing all roofs immediately. But eventually, if you say were to fast-forward to say 15 years from now, it will be unusual to have a roof that does not have solar. it's a fair statement to say that most houses in the US have enough roof area to power all the needs of the house.

Eventually, you can sort of roughly see that there's sort of a diamond shape overall, and when it's fully done, it'll look like a giant diamond, or that's the idea behind it, and it's aligned on true north. It's a small detail.

I think that first of all, I'm just on two advisory councils where the format consists of going around the room and asking people's opinion on things, and so there's like a meeting every month or two. That's the sum total of my contribution.

But I think to the degree that there are people in the room who are arguing in favor of doing something about climate change, or social issues, I've used the meetings I've had thus far to argue in favor of immigration and in favor of climate change. And if I hadn't done that, that wasn't on the agenda before. So maybe nothing will happen, but at least the words were said.

About space x this is one of our rocket boosters coming back from very high and fast in space. So just delivered the upper stage at high velocity. I think this might have been at sort of Mach 7 or so, delivery of the upper stage. That was the slowed down version.

we landed the rocket booster and then prepped it for flight again and flew it again, so it's the first reflight of an orbital booster where that reflight is relevant. So, it's important to appreciate that reusability is only relevant if it is rapid and complete.

So, like an aircraft or a car, the reusability is rapid and complete. You do not send your aircraft to Boeing in-between flights. configuration is about four times the thrust of the Saturn V moon rocket. This can take a fully loaded 747 with maximum fuel, maximum passengers, maximum cargo on the 747

I'm hopeful it's sort of an eight- to 10-year time frame. Aspirationally, that's our target. Our internal targets are more aggressive. While vehicle seems quite large and is large by comparison with other rockets, I think the future spacecraft will make this look like a rowboat. The future spaceships will be truly enormous.

it's important to have a future that is inspiring and appealing. I just think there have to be reasons that you get up in the morning and you want to live. Like, why do you want to live? What's the point? What inspires you? What do you love about the future? And if we're not out there, if the future does not include being out there among the stars and being a multiplanet species, I find that it's incredibly depressing if that's not the future that we're going to have.

I look at the future from the standpoint of probabilities. It's like a branching stream of probabilities, and there are actions that we can take that affect those probabilities or that accelerate one thing or slow down another thing. I may introduce something new to the probability stream. Sustainable energy will happen no matter what. If there was no Tesla, if Tesla never existed, it would have to happen out of necessity. It's tautological.

If you don't have sustainable energy, it means you have unsustainable energy. Eventually you will run out, and the laws of economics will drive civilization towards sustainable energy, inevitably. The fundamental value of a company like Tesla is the degree to which it accelerates the advent of sustainable energy, faster than it would otherwise occur.

So, when I think, like, what is the fundamental good of a company like Tesla, I would say, hopefully, if it accelerated that by a decade, potentially more than a decade, that would be quite a good thing to occur. That's what I consider to be the fundamental aspirational good of Tesla.

Then there's becoming a multiplanet species and space-faring civilization. This is not inevitable. It's very important to appreciate this is not inevitable. The sustainable energy future I think is largely inevitable, but being a space-faring civilization is definitely not inevitable. If you look at the progress in space, in 1969 you were able to send somebody to the moon. 1969. Then we had the Space Shuttle. The Space Shuttle could only take people to low Earth orbit. Then the Space Shuttle retired, and the United States could take no one to orbit. So that's the trend. The trend is like down to nothing. People are mistaken when they think that technology just automatically improves.

It does not automatically improve. It only improves if a lot of people work very hard to make it better, and actually it will, I think, by itself degrade, actually. You look at great civilizations like Ancient Egypt, and they were able to make the pyramids, and they forgot how to do that. And then the Romans, they built these incredible aqueducts. They forgot how to do it.

the value of beauty and inspiration is very much underrated, no question. But I want to be clear. I'm not trying to be anyone's savior. That is not I'm just trying to think about the future and not be sad.

References

1. lisa gansky: entrepreneur, author of the mesh.

2. wendy woods: social impact strategist.

3. Michael porter: business strategist.

4. Mallory freeman: data activist.

5. tricia wang: technology ethnographer.

6. tim leberecht: business romantic.

7. Alastair gray: brand protection manager.

8. scott Galloway: The Four: The Hidden DNA of Amazon, Apple, Facebook, and Google, amazon, 2017

9. Tristan harris: design thinker.

10. elon musk: CEO and product architect of tesla motors, CEO of space x.